HOW TO MAKE MONEY ON CRYPTO CURRENCY

Prasanth C

CONTENTS

Disclaimer

Crypto Currency Investments Involved Extreme Risk. Before Making Investment, Consult with Your Personal Financial Advisors. "Crypto Currency" Is Not Regulated by Any Government Authorities or Regulators, And This Is Not an Investment Advice Book. This Book Published to Improve Knowledge About Crypto Currencies, And Not Convincing to Invest in Crypto Assets. Any Loss Occurs on Your Investment Is Not Responsible by The Book Author or Publisher. "Do Your Own Research"

INTRODUCTION

Now A Days, We Are Living in Fast-Food Age. Every Day We Are Seeing New Innovations, As We Never Seen Before. Also, At the Same Time Job Losses Are Happening Because Of Disruptive Innovation. The Only Thing, That Never Is Change Is Changes. This Is Non-Written Law on Galaxy. Base on The Latest Technologies Climax, We See A Crypto Currency Innovation. On This Book We Take A Look "How to Make Money on Crypto Currency". But Before If You Believe Your Social Security Schemes Will Save You, It's Time to Stop the Believing's. Because the World Is Moving Not For "Youths" Age, But Moving to Internet AI Age.

Bitcoin

Bitcoin Is A Base of All Crypto Currency Innovations, Bitcoin Created In 2009 By Unknow Person, The Anonymous Name Mentioned in Bitcoin Whitepaper Is "Sathoshi Nakumotu". But No One Find This Person Anywhere. Anyway, Bitcoin Is Crated by One Human, But Even Him Think to Destroying Bitcoin Is Not Possible, Due to The Open Source Technology. So, No One Can Stop or Destroy the Technology.

Welcome to Awesome and Dangerous Investment

Crypto Currency Is the Most Volatile Asset in The Planet Earth. Due to This Volatility Crypto Currency Are Considered the Most Dangerous Investment. Every Coin Has A Two Sides. One Side Contain Risk, And Other Side Contain Reward. As the Rule of Investment Is "The More Risk You Take, The More Reward You Will Get." The Investors Around the World Is Getting Extremely High Rewards. Every Minutes Many Million Dollars Are Made Up by Smart Investors. This Book Will Focus to Teach, How You Can Become Smart Investor on The Crypto Industry.

EARNING METHODS

- Faucet
- Mining
- Staking
- Airdrop
- Investment
- Derivatives
- Arbitrages
- Margin Trading
- Lending
- Important Things

FAUCET

Some Crypto Currency Whales Is Running Free Faucet Websites, To Attract and Help to Understand How That System Works. It's Only A Small Amount Will Given to Peoples to Understand, How the System Works.

So, Don't Expect Big Money from That. You Can Learn "How to Create Crypto Wallet", If You Google It. Be Caution, Many Hackers Are Running Phishing Fake Sites to Stole Your Crypto Currencies. Mainly The New Comers To This Industry Was Heavily Injured by This Type of Scams. Keep That in Mind, On Any Investment You're Knowledge Is A 95% Investment, And Other Is 5% Only. To Make Sure You Want A Good Knowledge, You Can Checkout Many Crypto Currency YouTube Channels. Mainly "Sunny Decree, The Moon and The Box Mining" Are the Bitcoin and Crypto Influencers Are Running These Channels. You Can Easily Gain Knowledge by Just Watching Their Videos. But Books Are the Best Way to Gain Unbiased Knowledge and Opinions. "Never Share You Private Key to Anyone".

MINING

In This Place, Mining Not Refer Physical Activates. Mining in Crypto Currency Is "Verifying the Transaction Ledgers". Below the Paragraph You Can See the Mining Machine Image. Once You Setup and Started Properly, You Can See Running the Machine Automatically. This Machine Will Automatically Mine and Put Bitcoin or Other Cryptos You Selected to Your Wallet. But If Want to Purchase and Maintain the Machine, You Need Lumpsum Amount of Cash.

You Can Check the Mining Machine Price In Www.Bitmain.Com

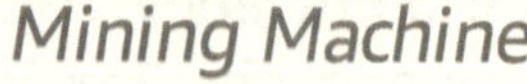

Mining Machine

Cloud Mining

Mostly The New Comers In the Crypto Industry Are Preferer To Cloud Mining Methods. Because It's Will Take All Expanses and Maintenance. You Just Receive the Net Profits from The Machine. Most Few Mining Companies Are Giving Genuine Profits to The Customers.

There Are Three Type of Mining Methods Available:

1. CPU Mining
2. GPU Mining
3. ASIC Mining

"Mostly All Mining Machine Are Running By "ASIC and GPU" Methods. But It's Cost Ton of Electricity Also. This Is the Main Reason, Few Countries Banning Mining (China and Venezuela)

STAKING

Staking Means Hold and Take Place on The Cryptocurrency Ecosystem. Like Stocks Are Giving Dividends and Voting Rights to Share Holders.

You Can Stake Crypto Currency From "Wallet" Or "Crypto Exchanges". Generally Staking Not Available to All Crypto Currencies. Mainly "Mining" Based Coin's Never Get Staked.

But Staked Coins Will Cannot Easily Transferred of Tradable. Mostly Staked Coins Will Take Unstacking Time up to 3 Days.

You Can Stake Directly from Official Wallets or Crypto Exchanges.

For More Information's,

- Www.Stakingrewards.Com
- Www.Poslist.Org

INVESTMENT

Investment Is Always Have Same Rule of Thumb, And That Is "More Risk, More Reward". Cryptocurrency Is Also Have the Same Rule. Many Crypto Currencies Now A Days Flowing into Market. Every coin Is Introducing Their Own Plans.

But 99% Crypto Currencies in The Market Will Eventually Will Fail, Due to Their Stupid Plans. Their Come to Steal Peoples Money. You Can Find Scam's with Your Own Research.

Always Remember, Your Investment Must Be Made Up by Own Researches, Never Invest Any Crypto by Other Refers or By Ad's.

Security Is More Important Than Investing on The Crypto Field. Because Cryptocurrency Are 100% Privately Owned by You. You're the Only Responsible to Your Money. No One Will Take in Charge for Your Money. So, Investment Are Your Own Knowledge's.

Holding

If You Hold A Crypto Currency for Long Term, that' Called Holding or Hodl.

Trading

If You Frequently Trade Your Crypto Assets, That Mean You Just A Trader. Trading Is Only for Professionals.

Note

If You Manage These Risks with Talent, You Can Make Money By 100 Time More Than Normal Peoples in The Traditional Markets (Stocks, Forex's, Bonds…Etc)

AIRDROP

Airdrop Will Be Given Out of Free or Bonus for Other Crypto Holdings. "Hard Fork" Is A Best Example for This Airdrop. For Example, in 2017 Bitcoin Get Hard Forked and All Bitcoin Holders Is Got Free 1:1 Ratio Bitcoin Cash Airdrop. You Can Learn More About "Hard Fork" In Google.

Bitcoin Get Many Hard forks, And Many Free Crypto Airdrops Was Given to All These Holders. Once Upon A Time "Bitcoin Cash" Reached and Even Beats Real Bitcoin Price for Few Minutes. That Was A Crazy Fomo (Fear of Missing Out) Movement at This Them. The Price Was 6000$ Dollars. Even If's A Free coin, It's A Jackpot for All Airdrop Receivers. If You Held 10 Bitcoins You Will Get Free 10 Bitcoin Cash. If You Think It's Not A Jackpot, Then I Don't Know What It Is.

Not Only Bitcoin, Now A Days Many Crypto Currencies Is Providing Free Airdrops. You Can Just Hold and Earn Those Airdrops.

In 2018, The Name Of "Ontology" Coin Is Free Get Airdropped to All Peoples, Who Just Fill Up The 2 Min Online Form. But These Airdrop Will Be Get Worth Of 3000$ Us Dollars In 2 Month of Time. Many People Not Used This Golden Chance, Due to Lack of Communication and Carelessness.

Like This, Every Day Crypto Gurus Is Earning These Airdrops. But Being Good Crypto Enthusiast Is Good for Your Investment Purpose. Many Crypto Youtubers Is Help People's to Get More Strong Awareness About Crypto Currencies and Bitcoin.

DERIVATIVES

Derivatives Is Most Risk-Reward in All Trading Strategies. Crypto Is Not Also Exempt This. Derivative Is Trade Based Leverage Method. But Derivatives Are More Technical Term. Derivative Mainly Are The "Future and Options" Contracts.

Futures

Futures Is A Guessing About the Future Ups and Down Trend in Prices. You Can Trade with Leverages. Correct Guess Will Get Rewarded and Leverage Will Multiply Their Profits. More Leverage= More Reward= More Risk. But as The Newton Law Every Activity Had an Opposite Activity. This Law Is Also Applicable to Derivatives. So, Futures Contract Have Same Risk -Reward System. Futures Are Created as Hedge Purpose Against Their Holding, And It's A High-Level Trading System.

Options

Options Is Not Popular Like Futures. But Options Is Techy and Hard to Understand Compare to Futures. Option Is Like an Insurance Against Product Damages. Options Big Advantage Is Limit Risk and Unlimited Profit.

Note

90% Derivatives Trader Are Only Losing Their Money. Derivatives Are Created for Hedging Purpose. Not for A Trading Purpose.

ARBITRAGE

Arbitrage Is Mean Same Object Is Selling Different Places with Different Prices. It's Hard to Determine the Arbitrages. Luckily If You Find These Opportunities, Before the Execution, This Price Different Will Get Adjusted.

This Arbitrage Method Is Very Profitable in Old Centuries for Traders. But Now A Days, It's Not Like Possible Due to Internet Explosion. Maybe If You Find the Opportunities," Arbitrage Software Bot" Will Trade Before You. Those Bot's Can't Run Easily by Individuals.

Problems in Arbitrage

If You Find Arbitrage Opportunity, First Try with Few Bucks, Before Leap You Leap your leg Full into River. Otherwise You Maybe Face "Wallet Maintenance" Or "Trading Halt" Issues.

Use the Fear

Human Get Extreme Knowledge as Never Before in Human History with Help of Internet. But Their Emotions Is Never Leave Them. Some Fake or Bad News Will Mostly Affect Those Asset's Price Due to Fear. At the Time Entering Is High Dangerous. But If You Handle This Situation. You Can Make Huge Chunk of Money at The Time. Different Places Have Different Prices, even "Arbitrage Bots" Cannot Handle This Price Fluctuation.

"Arbitrage Only for Professional's, Not for New Beginners"

MARGIN TRADING

Introduction

"Margin Trading" Is A Method to Borrow Money from Exchange's and Use This Money to Buy More Crypto and Sell at High price with Extra Profit. But Position Once Go Against Us, Losses Will Occur More Faster Than Traditional Trading System. "Margin Trading" Are Becoming Popular, Now Almost All Crypto Exchanges Providing "Margin Trading" Facility.

Interest

Interest Will Occur Every Day or Hour's Based on Different Crypto Exchange's. Also, Interest Will Be Differ from Every Other Crypto's.

Collateral

Margin Will Only Available, If You Have Collateralized Crypto in Exchanges. Based on Collateral You Will Get Money By 5x, 10x Or Even 100x Of Money. But You Cannot Withdraw Money from Exchange's. You Must Trade Internally on Those Exchange's, Until You Repay your Loan.

Liquidation

As I Said Before, Every Activity Has Opposite Activity. Liquidation Is the Process Against Profits. Liquidation Bar Will Indicate Your Profits and Loss on These Specific Trade's You Make. You Can Check Liquidation Bar on The Exchange Platforms.

Note

Before You Do Margin Trade's, You Must Read All Documents Carefully. Otherwise at Market Crash Time You Will Get Obligations for Their System Failures.

LENDING (SAVINGS)

Savings

Savings Are A Specific Sub Account's, Provided by Crypto Exchanges. You Can Call This A "Crypto Lending" Service as Well. Two Types of Deposit Available Here.

1. Flexible Deposit
2. Fixed Deposit

Flexible Deposit

Flexible Deposit Are Similar to Our Savings Account in Bank. We Can Put or Withdraw Our Money at Any Time. Every Crypto Currency Has Different Interest Rate. Flexible Deposited Interest Rate Are Always Swings Between the Range, With Crypto Exchange Decisions.

Fixed Deposit

It's Similar to Fixed Deposit Like We Do in Banks. It Will Provide Stable and More Interest Than Flexible Deposits. Also, Every Crypto Has Different Stable Interest Rates. You Cannot Get Back You're Crypto Until the Date Given at The Time You Deposit. After Expire Your Crypto Will Credited to Your Wallet.

Note

Never Save Your Savings Money Here. Crypto Exchange Can Get Hacked Any Time. So, Don't Put Your Life Savings There. Just Put A Par Money, If You Afford to Loss.

"Savings Method Is for Testing Purpose Only, Not for All One's".

IMPORTANT POINT'S
TO TAKEAWAY

- First Rule of Making Money Is Never Losing Money, And Second Rule Is to Follow the First Rule.
- Until You Sell Something, It's Not A Profit or Loss
- If You Made Investment's at Unwanted Times, You Cannot Made Investment in Wanted Times.
- Never Believe Anything, Until You Research About It.
- Securing Money Is More Important Than Making Money.
- It's Doesn't Matter How Smart You Are, You Must Do Wrong Decisions At Some Times.
- Never Share Your "Private Key" To Anyone.
- Always Have A Strong Leader's or Enthusiasts as Backup.
- Self-Investment Mean, Self-Profit and Self Loss.
- You Will Get Many Chances, Most of Chances Are Not Designed Easily Recognizable
- You Have Big Knowledge and Even Have Helping Peoples, But Some Loss Will Must Occur.
- Profits Mean Reducing Loss and Increasing Income.

www.ingramcontent.com/pod-product-compliance
Lightning Source LLC
Chambersburg PA
CBHW020946160726
47993CB00007B/2962